The Romans

The Romans

Pamela Odijk

Silver Burdett Press

Acknowledgments

The author and publishers are grateful to the following for permission to reproduce copyright photographs and prints:

ANT/NHPA p. 14; Bettman pp. 24, 26; Coo-ee Picture Library p. 35; Michael Holford p. 25; Mary Evans Picture Library pp. 18, 21, 30 left; The Mansell Collection p. 28; Peter Shaw p. 12; Stock Photos p. 41; Werner Forman Archive pp. 13, 15, 19, 23, 30 top right, 32, 34, 37, and the cover photograph; Stock Photos p. 41.

First published 1989 by
THE MACMILLAN COMPANY OF AUSTRALIA PTY LTD
107 Moray Street, South Melbourne 3205
6 Clarke Street, Crows Nest 2065

Adapted and first published in the United States in 1989
by Silver Burdett Press, Englewood Cliffs, N.J.

Library of Congress Cataloging-in-Publication Data

Odijk, Pamela, 1942–
    The Romans / Pamela Odijk.
      p.   cm.—(The Ancient world)
    Includes index.
    Summary: Discusses the civilization of ancient Rome,
including the hunting, medicine, clothing, religion, laws, legends,
and recreation.
    1. Roman—Civilization—Juvenile literature.
[1. Rome—Civilization.] I. Title. II. Series:
Odijk, Pamela, 1942–   Ancient world.
DG77.035 1989
937—dc20   89-33861
ISBN 0-382-09885-4   CIP
                                                AC

The Romans

Contents

The Romans: Timeline

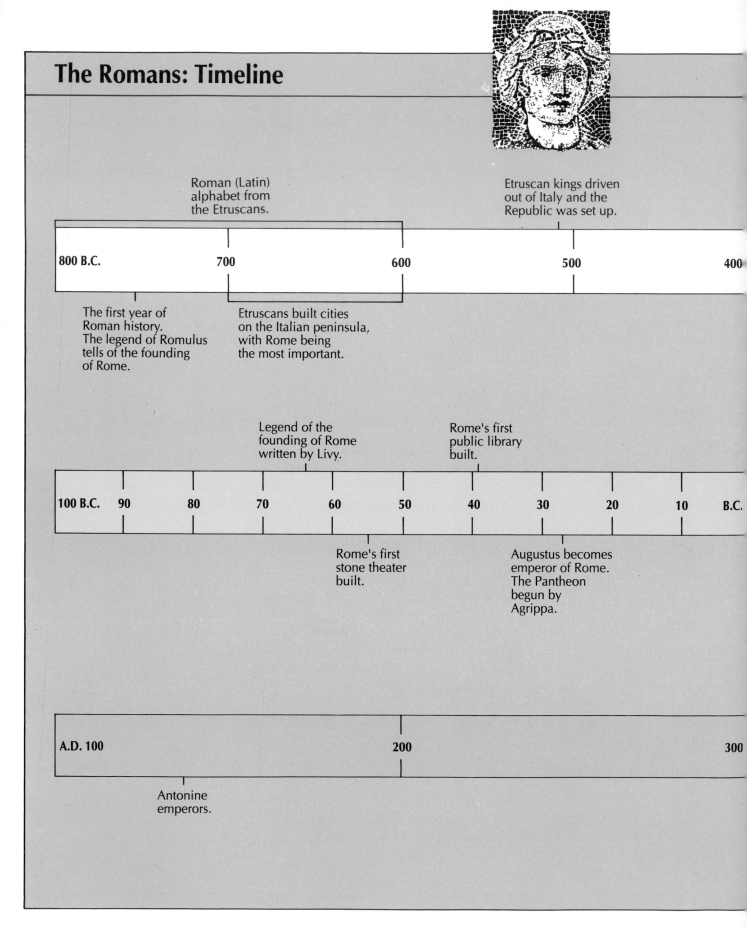

Roman (Latin) alphabet from the Etruscans.

Etruscan kings driven out of Italy and the Republic was set up.

800 B.C.	700	600	500	400

The first year of Roman history. The legend of Romulus tells of the founding of Rome.

Etruscans built cities on the Italian peninsula, with Rome being the most important.

Legend of the founding of Rome written by Livy.

Rome's first public library built.

100 B.C.	90	80	70	60	50	40	30	20	10	B.C.

Rome's first stone theater built.

Augustus becomes emperor of Rome. The Pantheon begun by Agrippa.

A.D. 100	200	300

Antonine emperors.

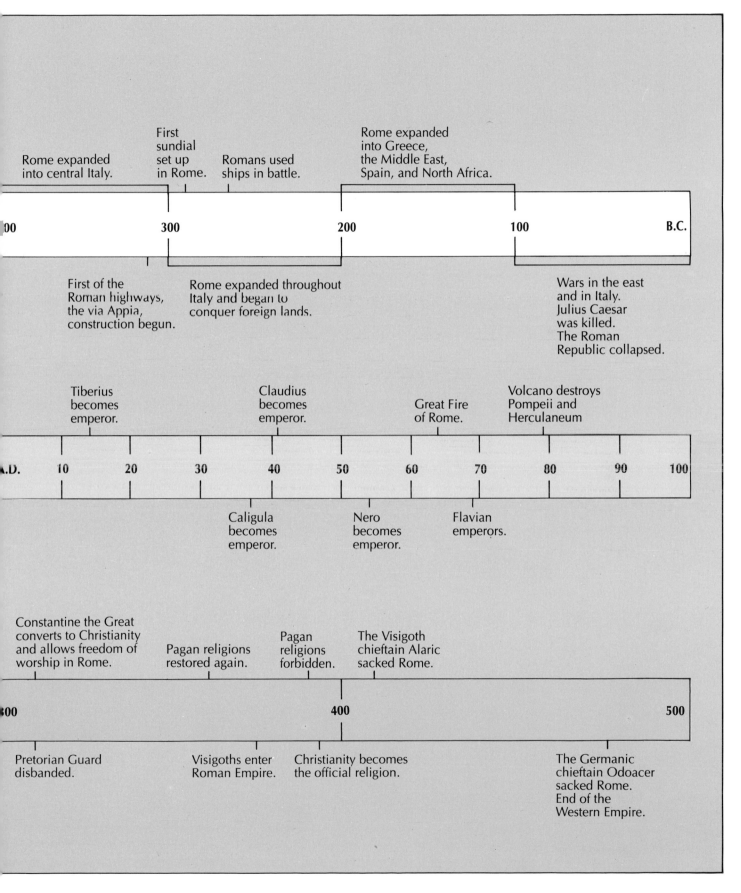

Rome expanded
into central Italy.

First
sundial
set up
in Rome.

Romans used
ships in battle.

Rome expanded
into Greece,
the Middle East,
Spain, and North Africa.

| 00 | 300 | 200 | 100 | B.C. |

First of the
Roman highways,
the via Appia,
construction begun.

Rome expanded throughout
Italy and began to
conquer foreign lands.

Wars in the east
and in Italy.
Julius Caesar
was killed.
The Roman
Republic collapsed.

Tiberius
becomes
emperor.

Claudius
becomes
emperor.

Great Fire
of Rome.

Volcano destroys
Pompeii and
Herculaneum

| A.D. | 10 | 20 | 30 | 40 | 50 | 60 | 70 | 80 | 90 | 100 |

Caligula
becomes
emperor.

Nero
becomes
emperor.

Flavian
emperors.

Constantine the Great
converts to Christianity
and allows freedom of
worship in Rome.

Pagan religions
restored again.

Pagan
religions
forbidden.

The Visigoth
chieftain Alaric
sacked Rome.

| 300 | 400 | 500 |

Pretorian Guard
disbanded.

Visigoths enter
Roman Empire.

Christianity becomes
the official religion.

The Germanic
chieftain Odoacer
sacked Rome.
End of the
Western Empire.

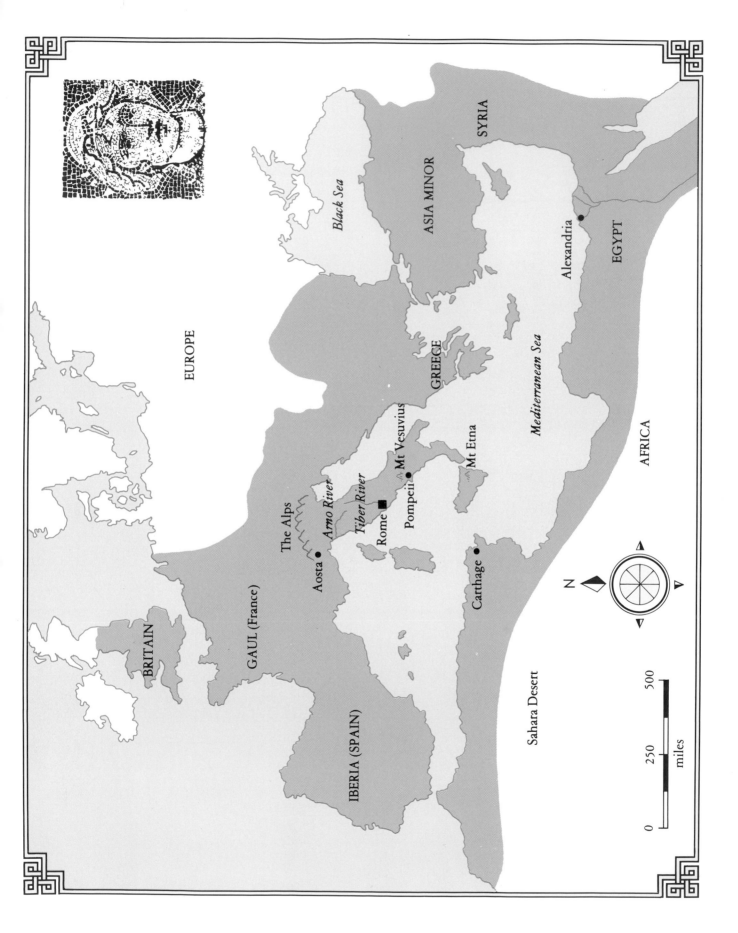

The Romans: Introduction

In the eighth century B.C., the earliest settlements of the Roman people, who were mainly herders, began in the Roman hills. In time these settlements united to form a city, which was ruled by the legendary Romulus, near the Tiber River. Between 700 and 600 B.C., the Etruscans from the north took over this region and built cities. Rome was the most important. In all, seven Etruscan kings ruled the Romans. In 509 B.C. the Roman nobles drove out the last Etruscan king, Tarquin, and declared Rome a republic.

With strong armies, battleships, and strong leadership, the Romans not only drove out all other invaders but conquered more lands. Eventually, at the height of their power, the Romans had conquered all the lands from Britain to the Sahara Desert and from Spain to Syria.

Over the centuries the Romans were ruled by various forms of government, from a monarchy (rule by a king) to a dictatorship (rule by one person other than a king) to a republic (where citizens elect their representatives and leaders). When the empire was at its peak, the **emperor,** who was called the "first citizen of Rome," was the most powerful person. Theodosius I was the last ruler of a unified Roman state. Upon his death the empire was divided into East and West.

During the fifth century A.D., people from the north invaded and occupied parts of the Western Empire. Rome itself was sacked by the Visigoth chieftain Alaric in A.D. 410, and in A.D. 476 by the Germanic chieftain Odoacer. Odoacer deposed the Western emperor, Romulus Augustulus, and set himself up as the ruler of Italy. The Eastern Empire (Byzantine) lasted until the Middle Ages.

From the eighth century B.C. to the fifth century A.D., the people's lives underwent many changes. They ended the practice of pagan religions and began the practice of Christianity. They built large public buildings, roads, and aqueducts. They established a system of laws, traded slaves, and adopted many things from the Greeks and other cultures.

Because the Roman Empire expanded in the way it did, Roman culture spread. Many things in our everyday lives have been passed down over the centuries from the Romans. They include the Latin or Roman alphabet and lan-

Roman coins showing the Emperors Augustus, Constantine, Octavius, and Julius Caesar.

guage. The English language has it foundations in Latin. Many English writers were fluent in Latin and, until recently, Latin was commonly taught in every high school. Roman law was the basis of the legal system of many European countries, especially England and France, and was brought to America by Western Euro-peans. So, too, were the Roman systems of weights, measures, and coinage. The Christian Church is based collectively on Jewish, Greek, and Roman cultures.

The main periods of Roman history and some important events are:

Important Events in Roman History

753 B.C.	The founding of Rome by Romulus. This is called the first year of Roman history.
509 B.C.	Driving out of the Etruscan king and setting up of the Republic.
300s B.C.	Rome expands in central Italy.
200s B.C.	Rome expands throughout Italy and begins to conquer foreign lands.
100s B.C.	Rome expands into Greece, the Middle East, Spain, and North Africa.
100–1 B.C.	Wars in the East and Italy. Julius Caesar killed. The Republic collapses.

Mt. Vesuvius explodes and destroys the civilization of Pompeii in A.D. 79.

Main Periods of the Roman Empire

The Early Roman Empire

27 B.C.–A.D. 14	Augustus, Emperor of Rome.
A.D. 14–37	Tiberius, Emperor of Rome.
A.D. 37–41	Caligula, Emperor of Rome.
A.D. 41	Claudius becomes emperor.
A.D. 54	Nero becomes emperor.
A.D. 64	The Great Fire of Rome.
A.D. 69+	Flavian emperors.
A.D. 79	Volcano destroys Pompeii and Herculaneum.
A.D. 138+	Antonine emperors.

Later Roman Empire

A.D. 313	Christianity officially tolerated.
A.D. 362	Pagan religions restored.
A.D. 391	Pagan religions forbidden.
A.D. 394	Christianity becomes the official religion.
A.D. 395	Roman Empire divided into Eastern and Western Empires.

End of the Western Empire

A.D. 410	Sacking of Rome by Visigoth chieftain Alaric.
A.D. 476	Odoacer deposes Romulus Augustulus and sets himself up as ruler of Italy.

The Importance of Landforms and Climate

The ancient city of Rome was located halfway along the Italian peninsula, a peninsula 683 miles (1,100 kilometers) long and, at its widest point, 155 miles (250 kilometers) wide. Two main groups of mountains are located on the peninsula: the Alps, with peaks rising to 13,000 feet (3,965 meters) in the north, and the Apennines, which extend down the middle of the peninsula. The Apennines are often referred to as the "backbone of Italy." Mountains cover so much of the Italian peninsula that only 23 percent of the peninsula is suitable for agriculture and grazing animals.

On the peninsula, many of the rivers are short, with some in the south causing widespread floods. The main rivers are the Tiber, on which Rome is located, and the Arno. During the summer many of the rivers dry up. In the center and north of the peninsula, many of the rivers are dry because the water which feeds them is frozen in the mountains.

Soils vary from rich volcanic soils to very poor limestone soils. In the past there were also active volcanoes, such as Mt. Vesuvius and Mt. Etna. Mt. Vesuvius is still an active volcano.

Roman settlements grew up around the pockets of good farmland. Because these settlements were usually isolated from each other, they eventually grew to have their own urban centers. If Rome was to conquer and unite the people, the settlements had to be linked by building land communications. The Romans did this. They even succeeded in building roads over the Alps. Rome was built on the Tiber River where the crossing could be controlled. The hills around Rome were suitable for growing market crops.

Climate

The climate varies from the north to the south of the peninsula. The mountain ranges in the north and along the peninsula affect rainfall. Most of the rain falls during the summer months. During the winter months, heavy snowfalls cover the mountains and foothills.

Opposite: Vesuvius behind Pompeii. Below: the Forum in Rome.

Natural Plants, Animals, and Birds

In the Alpine regions of the Italian peninsula (the regions bordering the Alps), trees included evergreen, cork, oak, European olive, cypress, and cherry laurel. In higher areas green elder and dwarf juniper grew, along with wild grasses, sedge, and dwarf willows. Forests of chestnut, oak, ash, poplar, plane, holm oak, olive, carob, and aleppo pine covered most valleys along the peninsula.

Animals and birds included marmot, ermine, mountain partridge, alpine rabbit, ibex, chamois, roe, lynx, stoat, and brown bear. Black grouse and gold eagles could also be found, along with various migratory birds passing through on their way to and from northern summers. Freshwater fish and saltwater fish were plentiful, and there were many coastal fishing fleets.

Ibex lived on the Italian peninsula in ancient times.

Crops, Herds, and Hunting

Crops

During the empire, part of the land was privately owned and part was owned by the state. The land was surveyed, divided up, and made available for small farms. Land for farming was allotted in **iugera,** and rose from 2 iugera in the fourth century B.C. to 32–50 iugera in the first century B.C. The original plot was called a **heredium** (a heritable plot). Large estates were broken up and made available to the poor. The original unit was usually worked by one man and his sons. Women usually did not work in the fields. If the farm grew, slaves would be bought to help with the work. Slaves had to be clothed, fed, housed, and kept in reasonable health. Slaves attempting to escape were crucified or chained. Town slaves were frequently sent to work on farms as a form of punishment. In some places there was large-scale farming using slave labor.

Mill and bakery at Pompeii.

The land was plowed, dug with hand tools edged with bronze or iron, and irrigated. Vineyards were established as vines were planted and supported on trees. The ground was thoroughly dug and fertilized with animal manure. Farming methods were generally good, with crops being planted in rotation and some fields being allowed to lie fallow. Crops included wheat, splet, barley, millet, beans, peas, vetches, turnips, and cabbage. Most corn was imported. Seed was sown by hand and covered with a harrow pulled by oxen. Harvesting was done with a sickle. Ears of grain were harvested first, and straw was cut and stacked later. Grain was threshed on a hard surface by having animals tread on it. Then the grain was sifted.

Herds

Raising sheep was one of the earliest occupations on the farms that developed along the Tiber River. Herds of goats, from 100 to 150, grazed in the woods. Pigs were kept, and pork was frequently served at Roman meals.

Chickens and bees were also raised.

Two writers, Cato the Censor (234–149 B.C.) and Varro (116–27 B.C.), wrote about the tools, implements, and labor required for various sized farms. The following example, from Cato, is based on a six-hectare farm. One hectare is equivalent to 2.47 acres.

Resources Needed for an Olive Grove

Equipment: 3 large carts, 6 plows and plowshares, 3 yokes, 6 sets of ox harnesses, 1 harrow, manure hampers and baskets, 3 pack saddles, 3 packs for the donkeys.

Tools: heavy spades, lighter spades, shovels, rakes, scythes, axes, and wedges.

People: 11 people including an overseer, housekeeper, 5 laborers, 3 teamsters, 1 muleteer.

Animals: 3 yokes of oxen, 3 donkeys to carry manure and 1 to work the olive crushing mill.

Machinery: olive crushing mill, oil presses.

Hunting

Romans did not approve of hunting as a sport for the nobility. This sport was left to lower classes and professional hunters. "Hunting sports," using captive animals that were usually imported, were carried out in the arenas of the amphitheaters for entertainment.

How Families Lived

Houses

There was a great deal of difference between the way the wealthy and the poor families lived. The poor were crowded into dirty, narrow streets and alleys where tenements, usually three or four stories high, had been built. These tenements were constructed mainly from wood and frequently caught fire. These poorly made buildings often collapsed. Building and rebuilding was always being carried out. Apartment blocks surrounded on all four sides by streets were called **insula.** Wealthy families had very elegant and elaborately furnished mansions called **domi** with sun terraces, courtyards with fishponds, and adjacent gardens and orchards.

Most people wanted to live in Rome in spite of the fact that housing was very costly. The cost of a house in the country was the same as one year's rent of a modest room in a cheap apartment house in Rome.

Roman houses were built as a series of rooms around a central courtyard, called an **atrium,** which served as a reception area. Slaves were housed in separate quarters, and men and women were given separate quarters. Children slept in the women's quarters. Early building materials were unburned bricks faced with stucco, but later kiln-baked bricks and tiles were used.

The streets of Rome were used as garbage dumps and sewers in many places.

Plan of a wealthy Roman home, showing the various rooms that led off the main courtyard.

Furniture

Romans had little furniture in the early years but as the empire grew, wealthy Romans spent quite lavishly on furniture. The poor had very little. In wealthier homes couches for dining, folding stools, women's chairs with backs and arms, and tables were the main furnishings. Early beds were high wooden frames with leather webbing for placement of a straw or wool mattress and blankets. Later beds were elaborately carved and decorated, as was most furniture. Clothes and money were kept in large wooden chests with paneled sides standing on clawed feet.

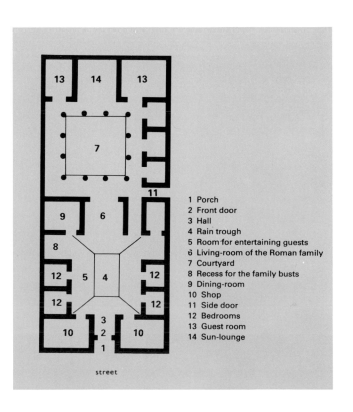

1 Porch
2 Front door
3 Hall
4 Rain trough
5 Room for entertaining guests
6 Living-room of the Roman family
7 Courtyard
8 Recess for the family busts
9 Dining-room
10 Shop
11 Side door
12 Bedrooms
13 Guest room
14 Sun-lounge

street

Walls were plastered and painted either yellow, black, magenta, or red. Murals were often painted on the walls of wealthier homes. Floors were decorated with mosaics. Lighting at night was primarily by lamps of olive oil.

Although the building of **aqueducts** brought water to the city of Rome, very little of this found its way into private houses, as few homes had indoor plumbing.

Men

Men were expected to marry and support a family. Penalties were placed on bachelors. Wealthy male citizens were the landowners in the country or became lawyers, political leaders, and **magistrates**. Magistrates spent most of their day in the city **forum.** Poorer free men were craftsmen or had shops in the **colonia** or market center. These men sold fish, fruit, and perfume. They also provided barber, cobbler, bakery, goldsmith, robe-making, and laundry services.

Men spent a considerable amount of time at the public baths, which were regular meeting places.

Victorian rendering of a Pompeii family scene. The homes of the wealthier people were highly decorated and spacious.

Women

Roman women were treated badly by society and the law. They had few rights. Women were expected to marry young and produce children. During the time of the empire (after 27 B.C.), marriage laws changed so that the bride's **dowry** had to be repaid if the marriage was canceled. This gave women a little more power.

Poor women kept house, cooked, cleaned, wove cloth, and attended to children. They may have had a slave to help if one could be afforded. Few women were educated. Because so little has been written about the ordinary women of Rome, and because few written records have been left, we can only learn about women from paintings and occasional remarks made by male Roman writers or **orators.**

Rich women spent their time being dressed and decorated by their slaves; going to the baths, the games, and the circus; and being present on social occasions. Also, wealthy women were expected to supervise the education of their daughters and the work of the slaves.

Children

Girls were not a welcome addition to a Roman family and were either sold or married off at an early age. Girls could be married at twelve years of age and boys at fourteen. Children were regarded as miniature adults or apprentice adults and were treated accordingly. Children of the rich were attended by slaves. Boys would accompany their fathers on their day-to-day duties and learn from them. By the end of the republic, many children were educated in schools where learning was very basic. Most Roman children went to elementary or primary school where beating with a cane was a common punishment for pupils, for all sorts of reasons, including slow learning. More privileged children received further education to become lawyers, politicians, or orators.

Slaves

Slaves were people who had been captured in war, born into slavery, or abandoned as children. People could be sold into slavery, and daughters frequently were. Slaves were bought and sold in the slave market. They had no rights and were at the mercy of the families who owned them. Slaves performed all the hard and unpleasant work and were punished if the work was not done satisfactorily.

Roman bed from Pompeii.

Food and Medicine

Food and Meals

The early Romans led simple lives. They ate very plain and simple meals of bread, olives, grapes, and honey. Wheat was the main food and was used to make bread, porridge, and pancakes. Fruit was also popular. During religious festivals or special occasions such as weddings, meat, such as pork and mutton, would be included in the meals.

As the Roman Empire grew, eating habits did not change that much. The first meal of the day was **jentaculum,** "the meal of the first hour." This meal usually included porridge or wheat pancakes, biscuits or bread with honey, dates, and olives.

At one time, **prandium** was the main meal of the day. In later times, the main meal of the day was **cena,** which was eaten when the day's work was over. A savory porridge made from wheat was also a regular food for poor people.

Wealthier Romans often made cena a social occasion. Dinner was an elaborate affair consisting of three courses or more, which were eaten while Romans reclined on couches. Tables were placed beside the couches and would be covered with salads, radishes, mushrooms, eggs, oysters, sardines, and sweetened honey. Fish, eggs, and wine were eaten during the first course. This was followed by the main meal, which consisted of lobsters, eels, chickens, and sometimes a whole roasted pig. Other meats that were often included were boar, venison, wild goat, mutton, lamb, kid, hare, and dormice. The wealthy Romans ended their meal with stuffed dates, sweet-wine cakes, and honey. Wine mixed with water was served from large bowls.

Slaves prepared, cooked, and served all the food. Often snow and ice were brought from the Alps to refrigerate perishable foods.

At the end of cena, which often lasted for hours, there would be a period of silence, followed by offerings to the household gods of wheat, salt, and wine at the household altar. Music was often played during cena, and after dinner entertainments included performances of dancing and juggling.

Those who had eaten simpler foods at cena often had a light supper called **vesperna** before going to bed.

Medicine

Before the Romans acquired Greek medical knowledge, early Roman medicine was based on herbal remedies. Salts were also given to sick people as a cure. The Romans relied greatly on the prayers and incantations of priests for medical cures. Various strange mixtures were offered to the household gods in a sick person's home.

Advances were made in Roman medicine after the Romans took over Greece. The Greeks were among the first people to study the causes of disease. Through experimenting with animals, the Greeks learned how to set broken bones and how to heal wounds. The Greek Hippocrates is today still the "Father of Medicine." One Roman nobleman, Aulus Cornelius Celsus, who wrote *De Medicina* in A.D. 30, based much of his knowledge on Greek medicine. He maintained that diseases should be treated "safely, speedily, and agreeably."

During the fifth century of the Christian Era, many Greek doctors went to Rome to continue their medical research. In Rome, some temples were turned into hospitals and medical care became part of the church's organization.

A Roman tavern (Victorian rendering).

Often, though, more attention was paid to the well-being of a patient's soul rather than to the illness. It was a widespread belief that disease was sent from God as a punishment for sins.

In earliler times, the poor could not afford doctors, and until the Christian hospitals were built, poor people rarely received the attention of a doctor. Common diseases included malaria, typhus, dysentery, tuberculosis, smallpox, anthrax, rabies, and tetanus. Plagues often spread, killing many people. Surgery was by trial and error, and there were no anesthetics, antiseptics, or antibiotics.

People suffering from dental problems usually had their teeth extracted. Wealthier people could afford artificial teeth made from ivory, one of the materials used for false teeth. Dentists did not fill decayed teeth.

Clothes

The clothes of the Romans were much like those worn by the Greeks.

Women

Women wore a tunica, which was adapted from the Greek chiton. The tunica was usually knee length. Over the tunica women wore a stola, which was full-length from neck to ankle, high-waisted, and fastened at the shoulders with clasps. The stola was usually either white, brown, or gray, though some were brightly colored with vegetable dyes. A shawl, called a palla, was wrapped around the shoulders and arms, or could be draped over the head. Cloaks were worn to keep warm.

Men

Men wore a knee-length tunic, either sleeveless or short-sleeved. Roman men wore a toga over their tunic, which was like a wide shawl that was draped over the shoulder and carefully wrapped around the body. A cloak was worn at night and during winter for warmth, and as protection against rain and wind.

Children

Children wore tunics with wide sleeves. Children of **patricians** (nobles/upper classes) wore a tunic with narrow stripes. When children reached the age of sixteen, the tunic was replaced with a white tunic.

Woman wearing stola and palla.

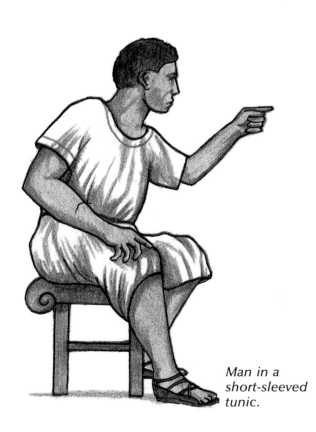

Man in a short-sleeved tunic.

Class Differences

Roman dress differed from one class to another. The tunic worn by **plebeians** (common people), herders, and slaves was made from a coarse, dark material. The tunic worn by patricians was made from white wool or linen. Magistrates wore the tunic *augusticlavia,* and senators wore a tunic with broad stripes, tunica *laticlavia.* Military tunics were shorter than those worn by civilians.

Togas

A Roman could tell how important or wealthy a person was from his toga. Free Roman men wore the toga instead of the cloak. It was originally an Etruscan garment worn in earlier times by both men and women of all classes.

Above: portrait of a girl with a tablet and pen.

The toga.

Child wearing a tunic.

The toga was made from white wool or white Egyptian linen. It was square or rectangular in shape and was draped carefully around the body.

The toga was often worn during state occasions. Consuls and senators wore a toga edged with purple. Some Roman senators wore white togas that were about three yards long. Some emperors' togas were made entirely from either purple or black cloth. Black togas, though, were usually only worn in times of mourning.

Footwear

Footwear also defined a person's position within society. Women wore closed shoes that were either white, green, or yellow. Men wore sandals. Patricians wore red sandals with an ornament at the back. Senators wore brown footwear with black straps, which wrapped around the leg to mid-calf, where the straps were tied. Consuls wore white shoes, and soldiers, heavy boots.

Cleaning Clothes

Cleaning clothes at home was difficult because of the lack of water and cleaning equipment. The task of cleaning clothes was left to **fullers**, who are shown in all paintings treading clothes with their feet. Clothes were also treated with sulphur and urine, and brushed with combs.

Jewelry

Most early Roman jewelry resembled Greek and Etruscan jewelry, but Roman styles eventually developed. The Romans were fond of colored stones, such as topaz, emeralds, rubies, and sapphires. Pendants, epecially cameos in gold frames, were popular.

Wigs

Wigs were worn by men as a disguise and to hide baldness. Fashionable women wore hairpieces that were often made from the hair of slave girls. Chalk powder, charcoal, and saffron were used as cosmetics. Men had trimmed beards or were close-shaven.

Hats were not worn except by slaves, but women were expected to cover their heads when walking outdoors.

Romans drawing water at a well.

Religion and Rituals of the Romans

The Romans wanted peace with the gods and to have their gods cooperate in all things. They believed strongly in the forces and powers of the gods, and regarded the unexplained as an omen from the gods.

The Etruscans influenced Roman religion, and so did the Greeks. As Rome grew, it adopted many of the Greek gods. The Romans also worshiped the gods of people whom they had conquered.

There were many religious festivals in which animals were sacrificed and games were held.

The Romans were very superstitious. **Augurs** were people who interpreted omens. They read signs to discover whether or not the gods approved of certain actions. The Romans also believed in fortune-telling. **Haruspices** examined the internal organs of sacrificed animals as part of the fortune-telling process.

At the temples high priests (*pontifices*) advised magistrates on religious matters. Often a government official would be elected as the chief priest (*pontifex maximus*).

The Romans came to have many gods. Every home had its own shrine (**lararium**) where daily prayers and offerings were made to the household gods. Each god was said to have a **lare**, the

Mosaic showing the four seasons and Neptune, who later became the Roman god of the sea.

personal or household effects over which the god has dominion. Some of the more important lares are listed below.

Gods of the Home	
Name	**Lare**
Janus and **Vesta**	Power of the door and hearth.
Penates	Spirit of the cupboards and home supplies. This spirit ensured that everyone had enough to eat.
Vesta	Goddess of the fireplace.
Jupiter	King of the gods; sky god. The Romans gave Jupiter his own priest (*flamen*).
Mars	God of war; protector in times of war. He was later identified with the Greek god of war.
Diana	Goddess of hunting; protector of the slaves and lower classes. Women who wanted children prayed to her. Her temple was built on the Aventine Hill in about 540 B.C.

A Christian martyr being led into the Colosseum. Early Christians were often fed to the lions.

The Romans also worshiped their emperors, many of whom were made gods once they died. Astrology was also popular.

Name	Lare
Fors Fortuna	Represented luck. Her temple was across the Tiber River, and was one of the few temples that slaves could attend.
Mercury	Messenger of the gods, protector of trade.
Neptune	God of fresh water, who later became identified with the Greek god Poseidon, and became the Roman god of the sea.
Apollo	God of youth, beauty, and music; the healer.
Venus	Goddess of love.
Cupid	God of love.
Ceres **Apollo** **Venus**	The gods of the republic.

Temples

Roman temples were built in a Greek style. Most of the temples were small, with front porches supported by columns. Only temple officials, such as priests and priestesses, assistants, and special guests, could enter the temples. Roman temples were used to house great works of art and sculpture, and treasures captured during times of war. From very early times, temples were used to house the state treasury and the money of private citizens.

Christianity

During the first and second centuries A.D. Christianity spread. More and more, the old gods seemed irrelevant and people began to turn to one God who would protect and save them. Christianity found great support among the slaves and poorer people. The Romans also worshiped certain gods, such as emperors, who had once been human. Therefore, the idea of Christ as a person and then as sacred was easily accepted.

In A.D. 312 Constantine the Great claimed he saw a vision of the cross just before his victory at Milvian Bridge. From then on, Constantine supported Christianity. In A.D. 392 the emperor Theodosius decreed Christianity to be the official religion, and the Romans were forced to obey.

Marriage Ceremonies

Customarily the bride wore a special wedding tunic, a flame-colored veil, a garland of flowers, and saffron shoes. Her hair was curled into six ringlets. A **pronuba,** or married woman, would bring the bride and bridegroom together and see that their hands were joined. After vows were taken, the marriage contract would be signed by fathers and guardians. Prayers and sacrifices would be made to the gods, especially Juno and Jupiter. A wedding feast would follow.

Death

Cremation was common until after the second century, A.D. Later, the Christians disapproved of cremation. The Romans buried their dead in **sarcophagi,** or stone coffins, which had elaborate carvings.

Wealthier people had funeral processions that included musicians and people carrying torches. A special speech for praising the dead, called a funeral oration, was given.

St. Peter's Basilica, Rome. As Christianity spread, Rome became (and still is) the center for the Western Church.

27

Obeying the Law

The first written code of law was displayed on the Twelve Tablets in the Forum. The tablets were written in about 450 B.C., and applied to all citizens, rich and poor, but not to slaves and non-citizens. Punishments were also written down. Today only fragments of the tablets remain.

The legal system and institutions set up by the Romans influenced the lawmaking process that exists today in the Western world. The law was divided into two parts, the written law and unwritten laws that were based on custom. There was another kind of written law called edicts, which were special proclamations issued by a superior magistrate. The Twelve Tablets were posted for all to see so that citizens knew their rights. The laws provided that a person accused of a crime was innocent until proven guilty.

Cicero attacking Catiline in the Senate, held in the Roman Forum.

Slaves

Under Roman law, slaves were regarded as possessions and were at the mercy of their owners. They could be educated and could acquire property in order to buy their freedom, but this was very difficult.

Slaves were often freed by their owners when food was scarce and slaves became expensive to feed. If the slave's owner died, a slave might be freed. Some freedmen and freedwomen eventually acquired property and important positions in society.

Family

The man was the head of the family and all property belonged to him. He had authority over his wife, children, and household. In later times the wife remained under her father's authority and retained her own property. Divorce was possible. Women could not plead in court. The marriage of slaves was not recognized under the law.

Property

Both land and movable objects could be owned, and often items such as animals and islands were owned by the first person to take possession of them.

Contracts

Contracts showing ownership or agreement existed. Originally agreements were spoken, but in later times, they were written in documents.

Courts

In early times, an accused person would be brought, first, before a jurisdictional magistrate, and then to trial before a judge. In later times, formal written instructions were issued similar to a charge. A magistrate would then hear these instructions. Different procedures applied to each offense, such as **extortion**, poisoning, **treason**, violence, and **bribery**.

Theft

The punishment for theft was to pay twice the value of the goods stolen, but if the thief was caught in the act, he or she would be flogged. There were also punishments for damage to property. People were imprisoned for debt.

Roman Government

When Rome set up the republic, it was called *res publica*, a republic. Male citizens voted and held positions in government.

Government of the Roman Republic

Officer	Position Held
2 consuls	Elected each year, one to serve as a minister for justice, and the other to control armed forces.
Senate	The Senate, which had 300 members, advised the consuls.
Emperor	The emperor was called "the first citizen of Rome." The emperor became the head of state when a new form of government, the Roman Empire, replaced the republic in 27 B.C. During the republic, the role of the ruler was defined, in part, by the military. Officers in the military were very powerful, even though they were not elected to office. During the empire, as the power of the emperor grew, the power of the Senate declined.
Patricians	Members of the aristocracy; they held voting privileges.
Tribunes	Elected to office by the common people, plebeians. Held the power of veto.

In 494 B.C. the plebeians threatened to leave Rome and start a new city of their own. Because the plebeians made up the majority of the population, Rome would have been crippled had the plebeians left. The patricians gave in and allowed the plebeians to elect two representatives called tribunes. The tribunes had an important power, the power of **veto,** which enabled them to stop any action of the Senate or consuls of which they disapproved.

During the period of the Roman Republic, the Romans became very powerful. By the second century B.C., Rome had conquered the Italian peninsula, northern Africa, Spain, southern Gaul, Macedonia, Greece, and Asia Minor. During the last Punic War (264–146 B.C.), the Romans took and destroyed Carthage in North Africa, a powerful city with extensive trade routes on the Mediterranean Sea.

By the first century B.C., Rome had become a very powerful civilization. But Rome suffered from a number of problems. The poorer people of Rome were discontented with unemployment and the lack of housing, among other things. Social unrest began to develop. The Senate was stubborn when it came to any social reforms.

Above right: sculptured frieze on the Arch of Titus, Roman Forum.

Right: Julius Caesar, 102–44 B.C.

Below: the Roman Forum.

30

Writing It Down: Recording Things

Roman (Latin) Alphabet

This is the alphabet used in the English-speaking world and in many other countries today. It was developed from the Etruscan alphabet by the Romans before 600 B.C. The classical Latin alphabet had twenty-one letters. This was further adapted during medieval times to produce a twenty-six letter alphabet.

There were two main types of Latin script in Roman times, capital letters and cursive. Some writing had a mixture of both.

In Roman schools, children learned to write on wax writing tablets with a pointed stylus. Children also had books which were first **papyrus** rolls; later, **parchment** or **vellum** was used. The papyrus was glued together and called *volumen,* from which our word volume comes. Quill pens were used to write on papyrus or parchment. Ink was made from soot and glue, resins, and octopus ink.

Shorthand

Although the Greeks used shorthand, the Romans did not use it regularly until the Roman Empire. Marcus Tullius Tiro invented the first Latin shorthand system in 63 B.C.

Books

Slaves, especially booksellers' slaves, copied books by hand. Booksellers sold new and secondhand books.

Libraries

Private citizens had libraries. Owning a library became highly fashionable. Rome's first public

Some letters from the Roman alphabet.

library was built in about 39 B.C. by C. Asinius Pollio. Emperor Augustus built two libraries, one on the Palatine and one in the Campus Martius. Rome had twenty-six to twenty-nine public libraries in these times.

Newspapers

Newspapers existed in the form of public notices, written by Roman officials. Then newspapers were posted in public places.

Calendar

An early calendar had 304 days. Nurma Polpilius added the months of January and February, giving a year of 355 days. This calendar was further changed by Julius Caesar to a year of 446 days and then changed back again to 355 days.

Sundials

To measure time the Romans used sundials. The first sundial was set up in Rome in 290 B.C.

Numbers

Originally the Romans had a system of numbers similar to that used by the Egyptians, but gradually the Romans developed their own. Roman numerals are still in use today.

Roman Numerals		
I = 1	VI = 6	L = 50
II = 2	VII = 7	C = 100
III = 3	VIII = 8	D = 500
IV = 4	IX = 9	M = 1000
V = 5	X = 10	

An **abacus** was used to make calculations.

A Roman sundial.

Measuring

The Romans adopted the Greek system of measurement but subdivided the foot into twelve parts.

> 5 feet = 1 pace
> 1000 paces = 1 Roman mile
>
> Roman roads were provided with cylindrical milestones, many of which have survived.

The sextarius (1 pint, 0.53 liters) was the basic Roman unit of volume.

Roman Legends and Literature

Romulus and Remus

The best known Roman legend concerns the founding of Rome. The legend was written down by Livy (b. 59 or 64 B.C.), whose books were a mixture of myth, legend, and fact. In the legend of Romulus and Remus, two abandoned sons of the god Mars were raised by a she-wolf. When the boys were grown, they set out to found a city. After escaping death, the sons asked the gods to give them a sign as to who was to found the city. Romulus was chosen. Later he killed his brother in a quarrel. He founded the city and named it after himself.

Unlike the Greeks, the Roman had few legends about their gods. Legends about the gods were adopted by the Romans, but these legends are not Roman by origin. Most Roman stories are about heroes in battle and how, occasionally, the god Mars was seen fighting beside them. Because women were not allowed to go to battle or to be leaders, and because they were not given much formal education or encouragement to write, we do not know what stories and legends were told by Roman women to their daughters.

Writers

Written works in the Latin language during the Roman Republic and Empire began as translations or adaptions from the Greek. After the fall of Rome, Latin remained the language of scholars, who were also fluent in Greek. Some Latin writers are listed at the right.

Famous Latin Writers

Plautus	Wrote comic drama based on Greek plays.
Ennius	Wrote poetry, drama, and satire. His epic poem *Annales* tells the story of Rome.
Livius	Founder of Roman epic poetry and drama. His main work was the *Odyssia*, a translation of Homer's *Odyssey*. Livius was a freed slave.
Catullus	Poet who wrote the finest lyric poetry of ancient Rome.
Lucilius	Poet of satire who wrote many books. None of his works were based on Greek myths.
Horace	Lyric poet and satirist.
Petronius	Considered to have been the first novelist. His work, *Satyricon*, was about society in the first century.
Cicero	Statesman, scholar, lawyer, and writer remembered as Rome's greatest orator.
Virgil	Greatest Roman poet. *Aeneid*, his most famous work, was still unfinished at the time of his death.
Ovid	Poet. His most famous work was the *Metamorphoses*, a long poem in fifteen books. His major poems were the *Amores*.
Sallust	Politician and historian who wrote about Rome in the first century.
Seneca	Author whose work became part of a collection of tales known as the *Gesta Romanorum*.
Tacitus	Orator, historian, and writer whose main works were the *Historiae* and the *Annals*.
Juvenal	Satirical poet who wrote about life in Rome.

Art and Architecture

Towns and Architecture

The Romans followed the Greek models and borrowed some of the traditional ideas of the Etruscans. Roman towns were well designed and laid out by Roman planning experts called *gromatici*. Towns had a central forum where business was conducted. Gradually commercial buildings grew up around the forum.

Building materials included volcanic rock and travertine (a type of limestone), which later gave way to brick and concrete. Marble was used mainly for decoration. Huge buildings were built for public use; others were built by wealthy individuals and given to the community. Slaves were used to do the actual construction. One of the most important Roman architects was Vitruvius, who lived in the first century A.D. He wrote a handbook called *De architectura* for other architects. This handbook was based on Greek models.

Romans built **basilicae** (public halls/court houses), baths, **amphitheaters, circuses,** temples, **triumphal arches,** and gateways. They made use of columns, piers, and archways, all of which were used on gateways, bridges, sewers, aqueducts, **colonnades,** and doors.

Roman temples differed from Greek temples. Roman temples had high platforms and steps and were built facing any direction. Greek temples faced either east or west. Some Roman temples were circular.

Some Famous Roman Buildings

Temple of Vesta Circular temple at Rome.

The Pantheon Begun by Agrippa in 27 B.C. and completely rebuilt by Hadrian in about 118 A.D.

The Colosseum Amphitheater in Rome.

Theater of Pompey Rome's first stone theater, built in 55 B.C.

Arch of Titus A triumphal arch which was built to commemorate the capture of Jerusalem.

Famous Roman towns where original buildings and streets still remain include Ostia, Pompeii, and Aosta.

The ruin of the forum in Pompeii indicates the size of the forum and the architectural style of the people who built it at least 2,000 years ago.

Pompeii was completely destroyed by the eruption of Mt. Vesuvius in A.D. 79 and remained buried until the eighteenth century when careful excavations were begun. Pompeii is a whole Roman town, perfectly preserved by the lava of the volcano. It appears as it was on that day when Mt. Vesuvius erupted.

Art

Statues were the most popular art form ranging from colossal statues to miniature statuettes. The Romans copied many Greek statues. Marble statues were often painted.

Murals were painted mainly on walls of houses. These, too, have Greek themes.

Mosaics were made from stone, glass, or terracotta and were used on floors.

Roman aqueducts showing archways, which were used in much Roman architecture.

Goldsmiths, silversmiths, and gem engravers, most of whom were Greek, made beautiful jewelry, vases, and other ornaments. Gold and silver were mined by slaves in Wales, France, Asia Minor, and Spain.

The great museums of art and sculpture were the temples. Here were housed the treasures brought back to Rome as war booty. Many fine works of Greek origin found their way to Roman temples, including embroideries, jewelry, furniture, vases, statues, and pictures.

Going Places: Transportation, Exploration, and Communication

Transportation

Romans either walked, rode in a litter (lectica) carried by slaves, rode an animal, or traveled by wheeled vehicle. Horses were ridden long distances, but mules and donkeys were used for short distances and as pack animals. The litter was used mainly by the wealthy for making short trips and visits in the city, but occasionally it was used for longer journeys taking several days. Wheeled vehicles consisted of a **raeda,** which had four wheels and was drawn by four horses, and a **cisium,** a two-wheeled vehicle drawn by two horses.

Roads

The Romans were the greatest road builders of any ancient civilization. The first of the great Roman highways, the Via Appia, was begun in 312 B.C. by the censor Appius Claudius to link Rome with military centers. By A.D. 200 a system of Roman roads stretched from Hadrian's Wall in Britain to the edge of the Sahara Desert and from east to west across the empire. Changing stations, where new horses could be harnessed, were placed at intervals of six to sixteen Roman miles and rest houses were twenty to thirty Roman miles apart.

Maps

The practical Romans needed maps to guide their armies and administrators. Roman geographers were also surveyors. Marcus Vipsanius Agrippa, a Roman general, constructed a map of the world based on geographers' surveys and the maps of military roads. Roman maps of large areas were drawn on a disk-shaped world, as these were easier to understand. Many Roman maps were drawn, but few survived the later Dark Ages.

Exploration

The Romans explored for minerals and trading areas as well as for military reasons. Often the Romans used the knowledge of earlier Greek discoverers.

The Emperor Augustus sent ships to India to bring back goods. In all, Augustus sent 120 trading ships to India. Other explorers ventured as far as Arabia. In A.D. 84 Agricola sailed around Britain. There are records of Roman expeditions up the Nile in Egypt.

Romans resorted to sea travel only when areas could not be reached by roads. Grain ships were 89 feet long by 30 feet wide and capable of carrying 250 tons of cargo and over 300 passengers.

Lighthouses

The Romans had built thirty lighthouses by A.D. 400. The most famous of these was the lighthouse at Ostia, the port of Rome. Other lighthouses were at Boulogne, France, and Dover, England.

Music, Dancing, and Recreation

Music

Music played a part in Roman light entertainment, religious festivals, theatrical shows, and processions. Music was played most frequently by slaves and professional musicians, many of whom came from other countries. Instruments included pan pipes, cymbals, flutes, and tubas.

Dancing

Dancing was regarded in much the same way as music. Although women were permitted to dance, this was usually left to professional entertainers. There were many people in Rome who made a living from singing and dancing, such as Greek minstrels, Syrian dancers, black musicians, and former slaves, who would perform in the streets, at the circus, at theaters, and at processions.

Marble relief of a magistrate responsible for organizing chariot races in the circus, a Roman public spectacle. Dated from second century A.D.

Theaters

Roman plays were first copied from the Greeks. In the theaters all sorts of performances took place, from serious plays, comedies, and mimes to a special ballet set to music called a *pantomimus*. In small covered theaters, called *odeons*, recitals of poetry took place.

Festivals

Gladitorial games began as religious festivals but became a separate form of entertainment. More than 100 days of the year were feast days dedicated to various Roman gods and goddesses. In Rome the number of festival days increased from 130 to 176 between A.D. 150 and 350.

Some Roman Festivals	
Ludi Megalenses	In honor of Cybele.
Ludi Cereales	In honor of Ceres, the ancient corn goddess of Italy.
Ludi Apollinares	In honor of the god Apollo.
Ludi Romani	In honor of Jupiter.
Saturnalia	Performed when the autumn sowing was over.
Caristia	For family reunions.
Lupercalia	Ceremony to honor the dead.
Quirinalia	To honor Romulus, founder of Rome.

After Constantine's conversion to Christianity in A.D. 312, freedom of worship was granted to all subjects of the Roman Empire. Even though the worship of traditional Roman gods and Christianity co-existed, Constantine prohibited the construction of pagan temples.

Gladiatorial games continued into Christian times, although the Church objected to them.

Recreation

Public Baths   Both men and women attended their respective public baths. These huge centers also contained gymnasiums, gardens, and reading rooms. Slaves would attend the rich, carrying their belongings, rubbing them with oils and perfumes, and scraping their skin with scrapers. Soap was not used.

Public Spectacles   These included **chariot** races held from time to time at various circuses. The biggest was Circus Maximus, which could hold 25,000 spectators. **Charioteers** were usually slaves or people from the lower classes. Chariot racing was very dangerous, and men and horses were often killed or maimed. The Romans would gamble on the outcome of these races.

Even more bloodthirsty sports took place at the amphitheater, where animals and people were compelled to fight to the death. Special attendants were at hand with ropes to continually remove the bodies of the dead and wounded. **Gladiators** were armed arena fighters who were expected to fight against each other and against captive wild animals. Gladiators were part of such spectacles from 264 B.C. to A.D. 404. At one such spectacle alone, 2,000 gladiators and 230 animals died. The amphitheater was sometimes flooded so that mock sea battles could take place.

The Romans also had board games and dice games for indoor entertainment. Reading aloud was also a form of entertainment.

Wars and Battles

Under the republic (509–27 B.C.), the Romans became very powerful. By the second century B.C., the Romans had conquered all the lands around the Mediterranean Sea — the Italian peninsula, northern Africa, Spain, southern Gaul (France), Macedonia, Greece, and Asia Minor.

As an empire, the Romans continued to conquer lands and establish provinces.

In very early days Rome had part-time soldiers who supplied their own arms and armor, and if they were rich enough, a horse. By about 100 B.C. a large full-time army defended Rome's boundaries. This army was backed up by a reserve army of the same size called *auxilia*.

War and military glory were part of a Roman's personal and political life. A young man was expected to fight and win, and would not gain political office unless he had been successful on the battlefield. (Rome's name, *rhome*, was a Greek word which meant brute force.)

Roman legions usually contained infantry, cavalry, archers, slingers (with **slings** for stone throwing), and charioteers. The medium armed soldiers, called **cohorts**, carried heavy javelins (**pila**), which could pierce the armor. Cohorts were the army's main strength. Cohorts were equipped with a short sword, curved shield, helmet, and body armor. They could also use their pila as pikes, which were effective against enemy cavalry.

Other weaponry included a portable giant **battering ram** mounted on a wheeled platform, a giant catapult that could hurl large stones great distances, and the **ballista**, a huge crossbow. The ballista had a bowstring that was drawn back by a **windlass** or a winch and could send **firebrands** into enemy ranks.

The army could construct lashed trestle bridges to cross rivers quickly, and build forts in the field in three or four hours at the end of a day's march. During long battles, soldiers would strengthen these forts and make forays into enemy territory. They could also march far and fast with all their equipment on the excellent Roman roads.

Roman armies were large, well trained, well disciplined, well led, and were paid regularly.

In peacetime the army lived permanently on the frontier. These military settlements later developed into towns. When the army was not fighting, the soldiers built roads, bridges, and aqueducts. They also built forts and walls to protect the border of the empire. Hadrian's Wall in Britain is one of these border walls. The wall linked sixteen major forts in Britain.

Prisoners of war were brought back to Rome as slaves. Any art treasures or valuables were brought back to Rome and guarded in the temples.

Pretorian Guard

These guards were special household troops of the emperor stationed in and around Rome and commanded by two prefects, or deputies, who were also appointed by the emperor.

Ships

During the First Punic War (264 B.C.) the Romans learned to use ships in battle and built fleets of **triremes** and **quinqueremes**, ships having multiple tiers of oars or many rowers. Roman ships had a corvus, or bridge, at the bow where the boarding party was located and used a **grappling hook** to make it easier for soldiers to board enemy vessels. Roman ships would ram the enemy ship and drop a gangplank, which, with the corvus, would lock the ships together so that the Roman legionaries could board and overpower the enemy.

Roman Inventions and Special Skills

The Romans had some new inventions and innovations. They also excelled at using and adapting the skills and inventions of other cultures.

Rotary Motion

The Romans used this principle on treadmills, which were used for operating cranes and other lifting equipment. A scoop wheel called a noria, powered by either water or animals, was used to raise water to a higher level.

Mastery of Iron

Iron was used in the Greek lands, and its use was adopted by the Romans. Hardened iron was used to make steel, which was fashioned into sword blades, knives, and agricultural implements.

Road Building

Roman roads were superior to all others. It is thought that the Romans adopted techniques used by the Etruscans. Main roads were twenty to forty Roman feet wide. Embankments were built to keep roads above the level of marshy ground or to improve the gradient. Bridge building was carried out with road building. Slaves maintained Roman roads. Built originally so that Roman legions and equipment could move swiftly, these excellent roads also assisted trade and movement of people generally.

Alphabet

The Roman or Latin alphabet was adapted from the Etruscan alphabet. (This topic is covered in the chapter "Writing It Down.")

Military Organization

The Romans were highly skilled at organizing and operating their armed forces and planning battle tactics. At times their opponents had superior weapons, but were defeated due to the Romans' better organization.

Aqueducts

Aqueducts were built to bring water from rivers to the urban areas. From 312 B.C. to A.D. 226, eleven major aqueducts were built around Rome to supply the city with water. Aqueducts were also built in Greece, Italy, France, Spain, North Africa, and Asia Minor. Most of these aqueducts were underground, but some also spanned large areas above ground using arches.

Bridges

The Romans were among the best bridge builders of the ancient world. They made major contributions to engineering and construction.

Central Heating

The hypocaust system made central heating efficient. It was used in the Roman baths and wealthy homes. The floor was elevated so that hot air from furnaces could pass and rise through terracotta pipes. The Romans were also the first to heat water artificially for bathing by using a furnace below a cistern.

Why the Civilization Declined

Scholars have debated for many years why the ancient Roman world declined. High taxes for huge armies, exceeding a Roman's ability to pay, may have been one cause. As the army increased in size, so did the taxes.

Others believe that even though the army was large, it may not have been large enough to defend the frontiers properly. Massive invasions of strong armies from the north could not be stopped by the Roman legions, especially when many invasions took place simultaneously.

Romans also appointed non-Roman generals to the army in later times. These people may have secretly worked against Rome. Also, jealousies and apathy in the government and army divided the people. They did not pull together to keep the empire strong.

There may have been other reasons, such as disease which may have weakened or killed many people. One of the greatest historians, Gibbon, thought Christianity weakened the Roman Empire.

For all these reasons, the Roman Empire, with its extensive lands, was gradually invaded by others until Rome, itself, was taken over. The old political and military boundaries were destroyed. However, the many buildings, roads, institutions, and other influences on our world which remain are evidence of the civilization of the ancient Romans.

Gondolieri, Venice — today's Italians are descendants of the ancient Romans.

Glossary

Abacus A counting board of colored beads strung on wires or rods set in a frame.

Aedila See *magistrate*.

Amphitheater A Roman theater with an elliptical shape where spectacles such as "hunting sports" and gladiatorial games, fights to the death, were held and watched by thousands of Romans.

Aqueduct A channel that carries water from a source, such as a river or lake, to a town.

Atrium The central courtyard around which buildings of the Roman house were grouped.

Augur One who read signs and interpreted omens for people.

Ballista A military machine for throwing stones and other missiles.

Basilica A large covered hall for the holding of courts of justice, banking, and other commercial transactions.

Battering ram A military machine with a heavy horizontal beam for battering or breaking down walls of buildings or ships.

Bribery The giving of money or promises in return for favors in the performance of official or public duty.

Cena Main meal of the Roman day taken when all work was done. It could be simple or elaborate.

Chariot A two-wheeled vehicle used in war. Chariots were also raced against each other as a spectator sport in Rome.

Charioteer A person skilled in driving a chariot.

Circus A large, roofless enclosure surrounded by tiered seats, in which games and chariot races were held.

Cisium A two-wheeled vehicle used for travel and pulled by two horses.

Cohort A group of armed men in the infantry.

Colonia Business or market center.

Colonnade A series of columns set at regular intervals usually with supporting arches and/ or a roof.

Cremation Burning. Usually refers to the burning of a body after death as an alternative to burial.

Domus A Roman house occupied by wealthier Romans. Plural *domi*.

Dowry Money or goods brought to a husband by a wife on marriage.

Emperor Absolute ruler of an empire.

Extortion A crime involving an attempt to take something (usually money) from someone else by using violence or by abuse of authority.

Firebrand A piece of burning wood or other material.

Forum Open-air marketplace where business was conducted.

Fuller Person whose job it was to clean cloth.

Gladiator A slave or captive armed with a sword or other weapon, sent to fight with an animal or another gladiator, usually until one or the other was dead. This fight was an entertainment for the Romans.

Grappling hook Also called grappling iron; a hooked iron for anchoring a boat, grappling ships to each other, or recovering sunken objects.

Haruspices Ancient Roman soothsayer who performed divination by examining the entrails of animals.

Heredium A plot of land that is passed on by heredity.

Insula A tenement or an apartment block in Rome occupied by the poorer classes.

Iugera The unit used to measure land (as we use acres). 1 iugerum = 0.623 acres.

Jentaculum The "meal of the first hour," or early breakfast.

Lararium Household shrine.

Lares Household gods or cherished possessions of the state. They were worshiped in association with the penates.

Magistrate An elected official of the Roman Republic. Two consuls were the chief magistrates. Below them were two or more praetors who judged law cases, two quaestors in charge of finance, and two aediles who administered the city.

Orator A person skilled in the art of public speaking. The orator had to master the topic, arrange the material, and deliver the speech. Each type of speech had special features and procedures which had to be learned.

Papyrus A form of paper made from the fiber of the papyrus reed which grew in Eastern countries such as Egypt.

Parchment Writing material made from the skin of sheep or goats.

Patricians Members of the upper class (aristocracy) from which senators were chosen.

Penates Gods of the household or the state. They were worshiped in association with the lares.

Pila Javelin.

Plebeians The class of common people in Rome.

Praetor See *magistrate.*

Prandium The midday meal, if one was taken.

Pronuba Married woman.

Quaestor See *magistrate.*

Quinquereme A ship or galley having banks of oars along each side, rowed by five men pulling the oar in a single wide sweep.

Raeda A four-wheeled vehicle drawn by four horses and used for travel.

Sarcophagus A stone coffin bearing a relief sculpture or inscription. Plural *sarcophagi.*

Sling A weapon mainly used in war. A stone was held in a pouch between two leather straps. The pouch was whirled around the slinger's body or head to attain speed. Then one strap was released so the stone traveled in a fast straight line like a bullet.

Treason Betrayal of trust or allegiance of a subject to the state (or country).

Tribune Roman official who represented the plebeians.

Trireme A galley or ship having three banks or tiers of oars down each side.

Triumphal arch An arch built to commemorate a triumph or victory in war.

Vellum A sheet of calfskin prepared as a writing material.

Vesperna A light supper.

Veto The power to stop an action of a lawmaking body.

Windlass A device used for raising weights and usually consisting of a horizontal cylinder turned by a handle. A rope is attached to the object or weight and the cylinder turned so the rope winds around it.

The Romans: Some Famous People and Places

JULIUS CAESAR

The best-known Roman is probably Julius Caesar. He was a Roman dictator and general who was born in 100 B.C. and died in 44 B.C. He was a prosecutor and a **quaestor** in Rome in his early years and became *pontifex maximus* in 63 B.C. and **praetor** in 62 B.C. For the years 61 to 60 B.C. he was governor of Spain. He became consul in 59 B.C. He led campaigns to Gaul in 59 and 58 B.C., and to Egypt in 49 B.C. Julius Caesar visited Britain in 55 or 54 B.C. He plunged the Roman world into civil war from 49 to 45 B.C.

He was assassinated in the Senate in 44 B.C.

Though Julius Caesar wrote many military books that have survived, his speeches, letters, and pamphlets have all been lost.

AUGUSTUS

Caesar Augustus was the first Roman emperor of the Roman Empire. His wife was Livia Drusilla. He was a capable administrator who brought about many reforms and made Rome the center of all political power. He also created conditions for peace, good communications, and a flourishing trade between Rome and neighboring countries. He was the author of a number of works including a biography of Drusus, poems, and letters. Unfortunately, all of his works have been lost.

NERO

Nero was the fifth Roman emperor and lived from A.D. 37 to 68. He had the reputation for being a cruel and extravagant man, with an unstable character. He was responsible for the deaths of both his mother and his wife. Although it has not been proven definitely, Nero has been held responsible for the burning of Rome in A.D. 64, and for persecuting the first Christians. He thought of himself as a good charioteer, poet, and lyre player. He was also interested in many religious cults.

The people became discontented with Nero's rule and revolts broke out. The Senate condemned him to death. Nero fled Rome and is thought to have committed suicide.

CATO

Marcus Porcius Cato, also known as Cato the Censor and Cato the Elder, was a Roman statesman, orator, and the first important writer in the Latin language. He fought in several wars, including the Second Punic War. Because of his legal abilities and his excellent oratory skills, he was given the chance to begin a political career. He was opposed to Greek thought and influences, believing that they would lower the standards of the Romans.

In spite of his many activities and works, his only piece of writing that has survived in its complete state is a Latin work on agriculture.

SALLUST

Sallust, whose full name was Gaius Sallustius Crispus, was a Roman politician and historian during the first century B.C. He wrote about political figures and practices, and influenced other historians such as Tacitus. Very little is known about his early life except that he was not born into the ruling class.

Sallust was expelled from the Senate because, it is believed, he argued with Pompey and he sought protection from Caesar, Pompey's enemy.

When Sallust returned to Rome, he was further accused of plundering his province, but he was not brought to trial because Julius Caesar prevented this from happening.

His works included *Bellum Catilinae (Catiline's War)*, *Bellum Jugurthinum (The Jugurthine War)*, and *Histories*.

CLAUDIUS

Claudius was a Roman emperor who lived from 10 B.C. to A.D. 54. During his time Roman rule in Africa was extended, and Britain was made a province of Rome.

When his predecessor was murdered, Claudius, who had the support of the army, became emperor. In A.D. 43, he invaded and conquered much of Britain. He introduced many reforms, including the judicial system and the availability of Roman citizenship.

He died in A.D. 54.

TACITUS

Cornelius Tacitus, who lived from A.D. 56 to 120, was a Roman orator, official, and historian in the Latin language. He began his career as a military magistrate, and held other important posts. He became consul in A.D. 97 and gained acclaim as a great orator. After A.D. 98 Tacitus devoted his life to writing. His works include the *Historiae (Histories)* and the *Annals*.

JUVENAL

Juvenal, whose full name was Decimus Junius Juvenalis, was a Roman poet. Not very much is known about his life: all we know about him is what he revealed in his work. He disliked corruption and pointless behavior. He is accredited with the sayings "bread and circuses" and "Who will guard the guards?" His satirical style was imitated by others, including Lord Byron.

THE TIBER

The Tiber River is the second largest river in Italy, and flows from the Etruscan Apennines to the Mediterranean Sea near Ostia. Rome was built on the banks of the Tiber. Some writers believe it was originally called Albula, but it was renamed *Tiberis* after Tiberinus, king of Alba Longa, a kingdom to the south of Rome. Tiberinus drowned in the river.

The delta area of the Tiber was prone to floods, which the Romans were unable to control.

ALARIC

Alaric was an Arian Christian, and chief of the Visigoths from A.D. 395. He led the army that attacked Rome in A.D. 410. This event symbolized the fall of the Western Roman Empire. Although the Visigoths plundered Rome, they treated the people of the city well, and only a few buildings were burned.

Alaric was a conqueror, but he sought land within the Roman Empire where his people could settle and live safely, and where he would be treated as a Roman dignitary. This did not happen.

Index

lares   20, 25, 43
Latin   9, 20, 31, 33
laws   9, 10, 19, 28–30
lawyers   18, 19
legends   33
libraries   31–32
lighthouses   36
literature   33
lynx   14

Macedonia   30, 39
magistrates   18, 23, 25, 28, 29, 43
marriage   19, 27, 29
Mars   25, 33
medicine   20
Mediterranean Sea   8, 30, 39
men   18, 22
Mercury   26
Middle Ages   9
Middle East   10
Minerva   26
monarchy   9
mosaics   8, 35
Mount Etna   8, 12
Mount Vesuvius   8, 12, 35
mountains   12
murals   18, 35
music   20, 26, 37
myths   33

Neptune   26
Nero   11
newspapers   32
numbers   32

Odoacer   9, 11
olive oil   18
olive tree   14
olives   20
orators   19, 43
Ostia   34, 36

palla   22
papyrus   31, 43
patricians   22, 24, 29, 43
penates   25, 43

plants   14
plebeians   23, 29, 30, 43
politicians   19
Pompeii   8, 11, 34–35
pontifices   25
Poseidon   26
prandium   20, 43
Pretorian Guard   11
priestesses   27
priests   20, 25, 27
public buildings   9
Punic wars   30
punishments   15, 28, 29

quill   31

rainfall   12
recreation   37–38
religion   9, 11, 25–27, 37, 38
rituals   25–27
rivers   12
roads   9, 12, 32, 36, 39, 40, 41
Roman Empire   9, 11, 15, 17, 19, 20, 29, 31, 33, 39, 41
Roman Republic   9, 10, 19, 29, 30, 33, 39
Rome   8–9, 10, 12, 17, 30
   buildings, 31–32, 34
   fire of   11
   founding of   33
Romulus   9, 10, 33, 38
Romulus Augustus   9, 11

sacrifice   25, 27
Sahara Desert   8, 9, 36
sarcophagi   27, 43
Saturn   26
Saturnalia   25
school   19, 31
sculpture   27
Senate   29, 30
senators   23, 24
ships   9, 39
slaves   9, 15, 19, 20, 24–26, 28, 29, 36–39
   clothes   23

houses   17
labor   15, 34, 40
religion   27
society   29
Spain (Iberia)   8–9, 10, 30, 35, 39
stola   22
sundial   32

Tarquin   9
taxes   41
temples   21, 25–27, 34–35, 39
theater   37–38
Theodosius   1, 9
Tiber River   8, 9, 12, 26
Tiberius   11
togas   23, 24
towns   34, 35, 39
trade   26
trade routes   30, 36
transportation   36
tribunes   30
tunica   22
tunics   23, 27
Twelve Tablets   28

unemployment   30

Varro   16
Venus   26
vesperna   20, 43
Vesta   25
veto   30
Visigoths   9, 11
volcanoes   11, 12, 35
Vulcan   26

war   10, 25, 27, 39
weapons   40
Western Empire   9
wheeled vehicles   36
wigs   24
women   19, 22
writers   16, 33
writing   31